TOUR
DE FRANCE

Published by Creative Education, Inc.

123 South Broad Street, Mankato, MN 56001

Designed by Rita Marshall with the help of Thomas Lawton

Cover illustration by Rob Day, Lance Hidy Associates

Photography by Allsport, Bettmann Archive, Duomo,

Darcy Kiefel, Wide World Photos

Printed in the United States

Library of Congress Cataloging-in-Publication Data

Berry, S. L.

Tour de France / Skip Berry.

Summary: Describes the history, route, and well-known

riders of the "world's toughest bicycle race."

ISBN 0-88682-539-3

1. Tour de France (Bicycle race)—History—Juvenile

literature.   [1. Tour de France (Bicycle race)—History.   92-203

2. Bicycle racing.]   I. Title.   CIP

GV1049.2.T68B47   1992   AC

796.6'2'0944—dc20

TOUR DE FRANCE

SKIP BERRY

CREATIVE EDUCATION INC.

On a July afternoon in Paris, crowds lined the sidewalks, leaning over steel barricades to peer down the Champs-Elysées. The famous street was empty of traffic.

Suddenly shouting erupted in the distance. Like rippling water, the clatter of applause flowed up the avenue, following the progress of a man hunched over the handlebars of a bicycle. Legs pumping like the pistons in an engine, American cyclist Greg LeMond pedaled furiously toward the Arc de Triomphe at the end of the block.

Greg LeMond.

After twenty-three days of competition, the 1989 Tour de France had come down to a nail-biting finish. At the start of this final leg of the Tour, only fifty seconds had separated LeMond from French cyclist Laurent Fignon. To win the Tour, LeMond had to have ridden each kilometer of the twenty-seven-kilometer time trial about two seconds faster than Fignon—a feat few thought was possible.

Laurent Fignon.

A staggered start had put LeMond on the road two minutes before Fignon. His face tight with concentration, LeMond sailed across the Paris finish line in a record-setting twenty-six minutes, fifty-seven seconds. But would it be fast enough? He hopped off his bike and stared up the Champs-Elysées.

Laurent Fignon, two-time Tour champion, was on his way.

HOW THE TOUR BEGAN

Since their introduction over a century ago, long-distance bicycle races have been as popular in Europe as baseball is in the United States. The first one-day, city-to-city bicycle race was held in France in 1869. Similar races, called classics, were soon developed throughout the country.

Tour cyclists pass through a village.

In 1903, Henri Desgrange, editor of the sports newspaper *L'Auto*, introduced a new type of cycling event to French racing fans. Calling the event the Tour de France, Desgrange designed the race as a series of six daily stages, spread over three weeks and looping throughout France. The winner would be the rider who had the lowest accumulated time for all six stages.

A quick descent.

1987 Tour cyclists climb a switchback mountain road.

Sixty cyclists showed up to compete in the 1903 Tour. The six stages covered 2,428 kilometers; some stages required that the riders pedal day and night to cover the distance from one point on the Tour's route to the next. In the end, a chimney sweep named Maurice Garin won, beating his nearest rival by a margin of two hours and forty-nine minutes. Garin received a prize of 6,125 gold francs, which was then worth about thirty thousand dollars.

Cyclists in the 1986 Tour.

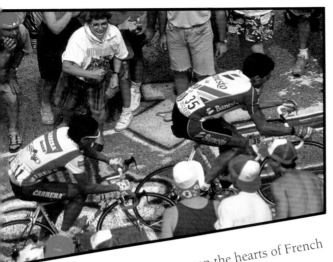

Over the years, many changes have been made to the race. The modern Tour de France takes more than three weeks to complete and covers about 3,900 kilometers (about 2,400 miles). The riders cover that distance in twenty-three stages—twenty road races and three time trials. Though the race route varies from year to year, the finish is always in Paris.

That first Tour won the hearts of French cycling enthusiasts, and started the tradition that continues today. Since 1903, the Tour has been run annually, interrupted only twice: from 1915–1918 during World War I, and from 1940–1946 during World War II.

Spectators urge on Claudio Chiapucci (Italy) and Miguel Induráin (Spain) in the 1991 Tour.

With the Arc de Triomphe in the background, the 1990 cyclists race to the finish.

Tour stages are held throughout France, as well as in such neighboring countries as Germany, Belgium, Luxembourg, and Spain. Cities or towns bid for the right to host the beginning or ending point for a stage of the Tour. From the flat farmlands of Brittany to mountain passes in the Alps, an estimated twenty million people turn out to cheer on the riders. And, thanks to satellite technology, up to a billion more watch the Tour on TV. Television crews, radio broadcasters, newspaper and magazine sportswriters, and photographers are also on hand, making coverage of the Tour de France one of the sports world's biggest media events.

Greg LeMond's teammates set the pace for him in the flatlands.

Gianni Bugno (right) prepares himself for a time trial.

GIANTS OF THE ROAD

Known throughout France as "Giants of the Road," the cyclists who compete in the Tour are the best road racers in the world. While they come from a variety of countries, they all share a common trait. Each of them believes he has what it takes to survive the grueling physical and mental demands of the Tour.

Not all of them do. While there are about two hundred riders in *le peloton* (the pack) at the start of the race, by the time the Tour winds up in Paris only 150–160 remain. Throughout the three-week ordeal, riders drop out for a variety of reasons—they get hurt in crashes, they get sick from heat or exhaustion, they aggravate old injuries or develop new ones, or they decide the pressure of continuing to race is too hard to handle.

Giants of the Road.

Tour stages vary in length and difficulty. The most demanding stages of the Tour are set in the mountains, and the most respected skill among riders is the ability to climb well. Every mountain and hill on the Tour is rated for difficulty, with the most difficult being the *Hors Categorie,* meaning "beyond category." The first cyclist to reach the top of a Hors Categorie mountain is awarded forty points. Less difficult climbs are worth fewer points.

In addition to points for climbing, the first twenty-five finishers in a stage receive points based on their final positions in that stage. While a rider's finishing position in the Tour is determined by his combined time for all the stages, his point total helps determine the amount of prize money he receives. A rider's Tour points are also added to points earned in other races to determine his world ranking.

Not only are the riders competing to win the overall Tour, they're also competing to wear one of five special jerseys. The most desirable jersey is known as the Yellow Jersey, which is awarded to the cyclist who finishes a stage with the best elapsed time for all stages up to that point. That rider is considered the Tour leader.

An uphill climb.

The next most important jersey is the Green Jersey. It goes to the rider with the most points at the end of each stage. The Polka Dot Jersey is awarded to the rider with the most points for climbing at the end of each stage. The Red Jersey goes to the rider with the most points earned during a series of sprints each day. Finally, the White Jersey goes to the first-time Tour rider with the best elapsed time at the end of a stage.

Climbing leader Steven Rooks (Holland) wears the Polka Dot Jersey in the 1988 Tour.

Panasonic teammates draft each other in the 1991 Tour.

Though only one rider wins the Tour, the race is run by teams of riders. There are twenty-two teams, each with nine riders and a support crew which consists of a coach, a trainer, and several bicycle mechanics. Every team is sponsored by one or more corporations willing to invest the millions of dollars it can cost to maintain a team year-round.

Leaning out of a car, a team mechanic adjusts a bicycle on the move.

Each team has a leader, the rider who is considered that team's best prospect for winning either individual stages or the Tour itself. Other team members are good sprinters, or good climbers. Those riders are expected to help the team leader by setting the pace for him during time trials and mountain stages. Known as *domestiques,* these support riders also relay instructions from coaches, and sometimes carry food and water to their teammates.

Whether leader or *domestique,* no one rides for a Tour de France team who hasn't proven himself worthy. To followers of bicycle racing everywhere, the Tour is the true test of a long-distance racer's skill, strength, and courage.

A domestique carries bag lunches to the team leaders.

THREE TOUR HEROES

The competition among two hundred skillful riders often results in unexpected tragedies and triumphs, and turns some riders into heroes.

One of the Tour's earliest heroes was French cyclist Eugene Christophe. While leading the 1913 race, Christophe broke the front fork of his bicycle on a rough mountain road. Because the rules of the time stated riders could accept no help, Christophe carried his bike twelve kilometers to a village blacksmith shop. There he labored alone to repair the fork himself, heating the metal in the forge and hammering it into shape.

A cyclist calls for a new wheel.

Because he had his hands full, Christophe asked a little boy to work the bellows to keep the forge's fire hot while he welded the metal pieces back together. Tour officials watching Christophe work penalized him an extra three minutes for the boy's help. Having already lost two hours on his repairs, Christophe couldn't make up enough time to recover the lead.

Rene Vietto had a similar bout of bad luck in the 1934 race. A former hotel bell-boy, the twenty-year-old Vietto was riding well in his first Tour. After winning three stages in the Alps and the Pyrenees, he was hailed as "king of the mountains."

Bernard Hinault wears the Polka Dot Jersey in the 1986 Tour.

But Vietto's luck turned when his team leader, Antonin Magne, broke the front wheel on his bicycle. Magne was wearing the Yellow Jersey, which meant that he was leading the Tour. Vietto stopped and gave Magne the front wheel from his bike, then waited for their team vehicle to come by a few minutes later and replace his wheel.

The next day, Magne fell again, and again broke his front wheel. When Vietto, who was ahead of Magne on the road, noticed his team leader was missing, he turned back. Finding Magne stranded as before, Vietto again gave him the front wheel from his bike. This time, however, their team vehicle was so long in coming that Vietto slumped against a stone wall and wept, knowing he'd lost his chance to finish the Tour with the leaders.

17

Raul Alcala, one of the top South American cyclists.

Still, Vietto didn't do as badly as he had feared. While Magne won the Tour, Vietto came in fifth—though by the crowd's reaction, it seemed as if he'd finished first. For his unselfish assistance, the crowd insisted Vietto ride side by side with Magne on the traditional victory lap.

More recently, fans applauded the heroism of English cyclist Paul Sherwen. During the 1985 Tour, Sherwen fell at the start of a 204-kilometer stage while trying to prevent a teammate from toppling over on a sharp curve. Sherwen lost his balance and landed on a metal barrier at the side of the road.

After Tour doctors examined him, Sherwen climbed back on his bike and started after the pack. The pace set by the stage leaders was too fast for Sherwen to match, however. With a badly bruised back and shoulders, it was impossible for him to ride properly, and he fell farther and farther behind.

Tour rules state that any rider who fails to finish a stage within a certain amount of time is eliminated from the race. Sherwen knew he wasn't going to make it within the time limit, but he kept pedaling anyway.

By the time he reached the finish line at the top of a 1,200-meter hill, Sherwen was more than an hour behind the stage winner—and twenty-six minutes over the time limit set for the stage. However, Tour officials were so impressed by Sherwen's determination that they refused to disqualify him. He went on to finish the entire Tour, ending up in 141st place.

A battered rider continues to race despite having crashed.

Pages 20–21: Cyclists round a downhill curve.

EDDY MERCKX

During the 1969 Tour, early in a Pyrenees stage known as "the circle of death," a twenty-four-year-old Belgian cyclist broke away from the pack. Warned by his team's coach to pace himself, the young cyclist responded by lengthening his lead. By the summit of the stage's fourth and final mountain, he was eight minutes in front of his nearest rival. Fending off all challengers from that point on, the Belgian went on to win the Tour that year. Eddy Merckx had arrived, and would dominate professional cycling for the next five years.

A fierce competitor, Merckx was known to his fellow riders as "The Cannibal" for his ability to eat up any advantage another rider gained on him in time or distance. He would stay in a race regardless of what it cost him physically. At no point in his career was that more evident than in the 1975 Tour. In that race he suffered two injuries, either of which would have eliminated an ordinary rider.

Belgian cyclist Eddy Merckx in the 1969 Tour.

First, during a mountain stage, Merckx was punched by a French fan who later claimed he'd been waving when he accidentally struck the Belgian champion. Accident or not, the incident left Merckx with a painfully bruised liver, which made riding difficult.

A grueling mountain stage.

Days later, Merckx fell and fractured his jaw. But when Tour doctors told him to quit the race, he refused. Though obviously in pain from both his injuries, he rode the final five stages, chasing the leader Bernard Thevenet the entire time. Entering Paris less than three minutes behind Thevenet at the Tour's end, Merckx said that if he'd quit, Thevenet's victory wouldn't have seemed as great as it was.

In all, Merckx rode in seven Tours and won five, earning a reputation as one of the greatest cyclists in history.

France's rising star, Charles Mottet, in the 1991 Tour.

BERNARD HINAULT

Merckx retired from racing in 1978, just a few months before a twenty-three-year-old French cyclist named Bernard Hinault won his first Tour. Hailed by the press as the next Merckx, Hinault's main talent was his ability to do well in time trials. That ability, plus his drive to win, would earn him five Tour victories in his racing career.

The son of a poor Breton farmer, Hinault first rode a bicycle for transportation; his family didn't own a car. When he later took up racing, long-distance riding came naturally to him.

Known among cyclists as "The Badger" for his ferocious desire to win and his refusal to give up even under the worst of conditions, Hinault was also one of the road racing's most wily riders. A rival once said that Hinault not only outpedaled his competitors, he outthought them as well.

A bad knee forced Hinault to quit the 1980 Tour, but he returned the following year to win the race by fourteen and a half minutes. That was the largest margin of victory since Merckx's eight-minute margin in 1969. Not only did Hinault win the 1981 Tour, he set a record average speed of thirty-eight kilometers an hour (about twenty-four miles per hour).

In 1982 Hinault once again won the Tour, running up his total to four victories. But in 1983, knee surgery forced him to miss the race, and made the French media declare that a fifth win seemed unlikely. That was a challenge Hinault couldn't ignore.

Though he lost the 1984 Tour to teammate Laurent Fignon, Hinault set his sights on winning in 1985. A fall during a time trial partway through the Tour broke his nose and almost cost him the race. Hinault's will to win kept him riding in spite of breathing difficulties that resulted from his injury. In the end, he overcame both his broken nose and his challengers to win his fifth Tour.

Bernard Hinault (left) and Laurent Fignon (right).

As great as his earlier triumphs were, Hinault is best remembered for his last great triumph. Before retiring in 1986, Hinault selected his successor. Then he tried his best to beat him.

Cycling enthusiasts crowd together to cheer on the riders.

Greg LeMond rides with Bernard Hinault.

The rider Hinault saw as having the talent and ability to succeed him as a champion cyclist was a young American teammate whom he promised to help win the 1986 Tour. However, in the first mountain stage of the race, Hinault staged a one-man breakaway. Opening a gap between himself and the pack, Hinault left behind the teammate he'd vowed to assist. Feeling betrayed, but bound by the unwritten rule that forbids one teammate from racing against another, the American didn't pursue Hinault.

The seventeenth stage of the 1986 Tour.

The next day, when fatigue sapped him of his drive partway through a four-mountain stage, Hinault told his young teammate to take the lead. But when the younger rider did, Hinault's pride prompted him to respond. The Tour became a cat-and-mouse game between the two teammates, and the pace they set left most of the pack in the dust.

In the end, that pace forced even Hinault to slack off. Three days before the final stage, he publicly declared the battle finished, and threw his support behind his teammate. He'd pressed as hard as he had, said Hinault, to find out if the young rider was good enough to be a Tour champion. He was.

Hinault's teammate rode into Paris victorious. And Hinault rode in triumphant, too, having proven that The Badger was as wily as ever. The rider Hinault dueled with was Greg LeMond.

GREG LEMOND

When Greg LeMond crossed the finish line in Paris in 1986, he did more than win his first Tour. He became the first American to win the race. Until that victory, few Americans had even ridden in the Tour.

While LeMond's first win was a dramatic moment, what followed was even more so. Less than a year after winning the 1986 Tour, LeMond was accidentally shot while hunting. With more than sixty shotgun pellets in his back, he nearly died from shock and loss of blood before he got to a hospital.

Pedro Delgado (Spain), winner of the 1988 Tour.

Page 29: Miguel Induráin (Spain), 1991 Tour winner.

For months afterward, LeMond struggled to recover his strength and stamina. No sooner was he up and around than he had to have emergency surgery to remove an inflamed appendix. By the time he finally returned to racing in late 1988, LeMond had lost both his physical abilities and his confidence.

He entered a few races in early 1989, finishing well down in the rankings. Among the top six hundred riders in the world, LeMond had fallen from second to sixty-ninth. But his riding gradually improved as he regained his competitive spirit.

In 1989, two years after being shot, LeMond decided he was ready to try the Tour again. He expected to ride well, but not to win. Being back on the road, however, fanned his competitive spark, and he found himself in a battle with Laurent Fignon for the Yellow Jersey. By the final time of the race, the two men were pitted against the clock for the Tour championship.

Since riding together on the same team in the early 1980s, LeMond and Fignon had developed a relationship based on respect for each other's abilities. That respect was well founded: They'd both won the Tour. Fignon had won it twice, in fact. And when LeMond had been shot, Fignon had been the only European rider to send his condolences. The two cyclists weren't friends, but they were respectful rivals.

Now that rivalry had come down to the tightest finish in Tour history. Fignon was confident that his third Tour championship was in hand, but he knew that LeMond was a skillful rider, and that the fifty seconds separating them didn't guarantee Fignon victory.

Greg LeMond on the comeback trail.

Erik Breukink (Holland) competes in a 1991 time trial.

By the time he entered Paris, the situation looked grim. And by the time he passed the Arc de Triomphe, the race was over. Fignon crossed the finish line with a time of twenty-seven minutes, fifty-five seconds—fifty-eight seconds slower than LeMond, and eight seconds too slow to win.

LeMond had just won his second Tour de France!

While there have been many great moments in Tour de France history, none has topped those final minutes of the 1989 Tour.

A strong sprinter, Fignon roared over the course, his blond ponytail flapping behind him like the tail of a racehorse. His support crew kept him informed of Le-Mond's progress as well as his own. The news wasn't good. While LeMond was miraculously making up the time he needed, Fignon was losing precious seconds.

Fignon races against the clock.

The victory goes to LeMond.